MY NAME IS JoJo

By Mommy (Nastasja K)

Told by me... JoJo!

Illustrated by **Breeliance**

Copyright © 2025 by Nastasja K. Douglass All rights reserved.

No part of this book may be reproduced, stored in a retrieval system, or transmitted in any form or by any means without the prior written permission of the publisher or author, except for brief quotations used in reviews or articles.

Text by Nastasja K. Douglas
Illustrations by Breeliance
Editing and Design by Pamela D. Cox
Publishing Support provided by PCox Enterprises

ISBN: 9798999424808 (Hardback)
ISBN: 9798999424815 (Paperback)
ISBN: 9798999424822 (EBook)

First Edition
Printed in the United States of America.

THIS BOOK BELONGS TO:

_____

My Name is JoJo gives readers a peek into how JoJo experiences the world-his joy, his sensitivity, and the way his brain works like a superhero's. Loud noises might hurt, and school might feel confusing, but JoJo's story isn't about struggle -it's about understanding.

This book gently opens the door to autism awareness, showing that different doesn't mean less.

It means powerful.

It means unique.

It means JoJo.

Hi. My name is JoJo. I'm six years old.
I like sonic toys, goldfish, and spinning in
circles until I fall down laughing.
I'm really good at remembering things…
even stuff mommy and daddy forget.

Sometimes people say I'm different. I hear words like
Autism and "spet-ram" (I think that's how you say it,
but nobody asked me what that means to me.)

To me?
It means my brain is like a superhero's brain.
That's what Josie says. She helps me talk about my feelings…
and she's my best friend.

She says I see stuff other people don't.
Like…sometimes I hear music in the wind.
And I see colors when people talk.
And I can hear the lights buzzing. Can you hear that too?

But loud noises hurt my ears, and big crowds make my tummy feel
funny. So sometimes, I need to go somewhere quiet —
and that's okay. Josie says taking breaks is good.
She says listening to my body is my superpower.
And I think she's right.

But not everyone gets it.
Some schools said "No" before they even got to know me.
One school let me in. But when graduation came... they left me out.
Even though I practiced.
Even though I showed up.

That day, my heart felt squished. I wanted to wear the cap.
I wanted to clap for friends. I wanted to say, "I did it!"
But instead, I stayed home.
I asked Mommy, "Why didn't they invite me?"
This book is my way of answering that.
For me. For kids like me. For everyone who's ever felt like the only one.
Because I'm JoJo. And just because I do things my way —
doesn't mean it's the wrong way. It just means it's mine.

-Before School-

Before school, I only went to a place with soft floors and nice ladies who played games with me. It's called services, but to me, it just feels like playing.
There are no bells. No loud kids. No big rules. Just me, my best friend Josie, and some puzzles. But then Mama said, "JoJo, you're a big boy now. It's time for real school."
I didn't feel big. I felt... wobbly inside. Like Jell-O. That morning, mommy laid out my favorite Thomas the Train shirt, the one with the big Thomas.
Did I tell you I like trains?
Mama packed my lunch and smiled real big, even though I think her eyes were sad.

-First Day of School-

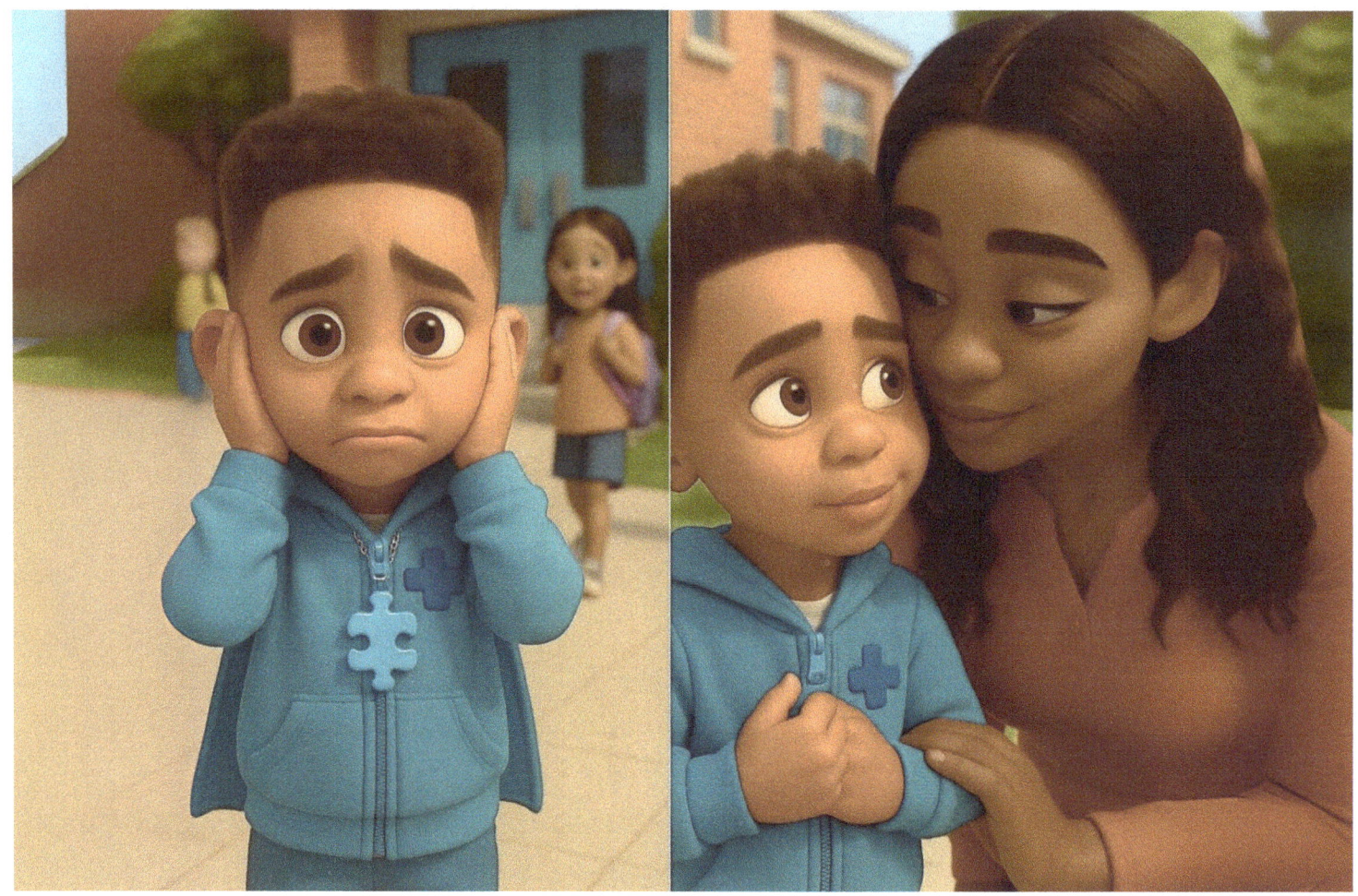

When we got to the school, there were kids everywhere!

Running. Shouting. Laughing too loud.

**I covered my ears. My hands got sweaty. I wanted to go home.
But Mama knelt down and said, "JoJo, you're not alone.
I'm always with you, even when I'm not right next to you."
Then she kissed my forehead and whispered, "You've got this, baby."**

I had mac and cheese for lunch. The teacher gave me a fork,
but my fingers said no. They get tired easy, and stuff falls out.
So, I used my hands. It was messy. Like... really messy.
Some kids were whispering. But I didn't care.
Maybe they never saw a superhero eat before.
Cause I'm JoJo. And I do things my way.

Inside the classroom,
everything was new.

The chairs were cold.
The lights were too bright.

There were rules I didn't
understand, like
"Raise your hand." and
"No spinning in circles."

I sat in the corner for a while...
Just watching.

And you know what?
That was okay.

The teacher smiled and said,
**"You don't have to talk yet, JoJo.
Just be you."**

So, I did.

I lined up all the crayons by color.

I counted the ceiling tiles (there were 47).

When the other kids colored the sun yellow,

I made mine blue—

because sometimes,

the sun feels blue.

That was my first day of real school.

I didn't talk much.

But I showed up.

And that's brave, too.

-My Brain Works Different-

"You were made to shine"

Sometimes people say, "JoJo, you're not like the other kids."
And I don't really know what they mean.
But I know I feel things different.
I hear things louder.
Lights are brighter.
Smells are smell-ier.

My brain is always on.
Like a superhero power button that never turns off.

Josie says that's called autism.
But to me, it just means my brain is doing cool stuff.
Like it sees patterns in the floor.
Or hears music in the wind.
Or remembers everything… even stuff nobody else notices.

Sometimes I forget things like zipping my backpack.
I always remember the sound geese make when they're close.
Did I tell you I like geese?

But sometimes people don't understand me.
One day, I was flapping my hands because I was excited.

A boy laughed and said,
"Why do you do that? You look weird."

That made my tummy feel twisty.
I didn't know how to answer.
So, I didn't.

Later, Mama said,
**"Your brain is a beautiful place, baby.
Not everyone will understand it—and that's okay.
You were made to shine, not to shrink."**

So now when I flap, I say,
"I'm just flying a little."
Because sometimes, my feelings are too big to stay still.

-The Day I Got Overwhelmed-

Today, my brain felt too full. Like when you pour too much
juice in a cup and it spills all over the table. Yeah... like that.
It started with the fire alarm. **BEEP BEEP BEEP!**
It was loud and scary, and I didn't know where to go.
The teacher said, "Line up!" But my feet wouldn't move.
My ears hurt. My heart got fast. And I dropped my blue crayon on the floor.
Did I tell you I like blue crayons with glitter?

I tried to hold it in. But I couldn't.
I covered my ears and sat down.
Right there in the middle of the classroom.

Some kids looked at me. One girl laughed a little.
But I didn't care. I couldn't.
Because my body felt like it was shaking on the inside,
even if it wasn't on the outside.

The teacher came and sat next to me.
She didn't say much. Just gave me her quiet and that helped.

Later, I sat in a room with soft pillows.
Josie used to call it my "peace place."
I like that name.

When Mama picked me up,
I told her everything.
She didn't get mad.

She said, "Baby, sometimes the world is too loud.
You're allowed to pause. You're allowed to protect your peace."

So now I know.
Sometimes I get overwhelmed.
And that's not bad.
That's just my brain saying,
I need a minute.

-When I Made a Friend-

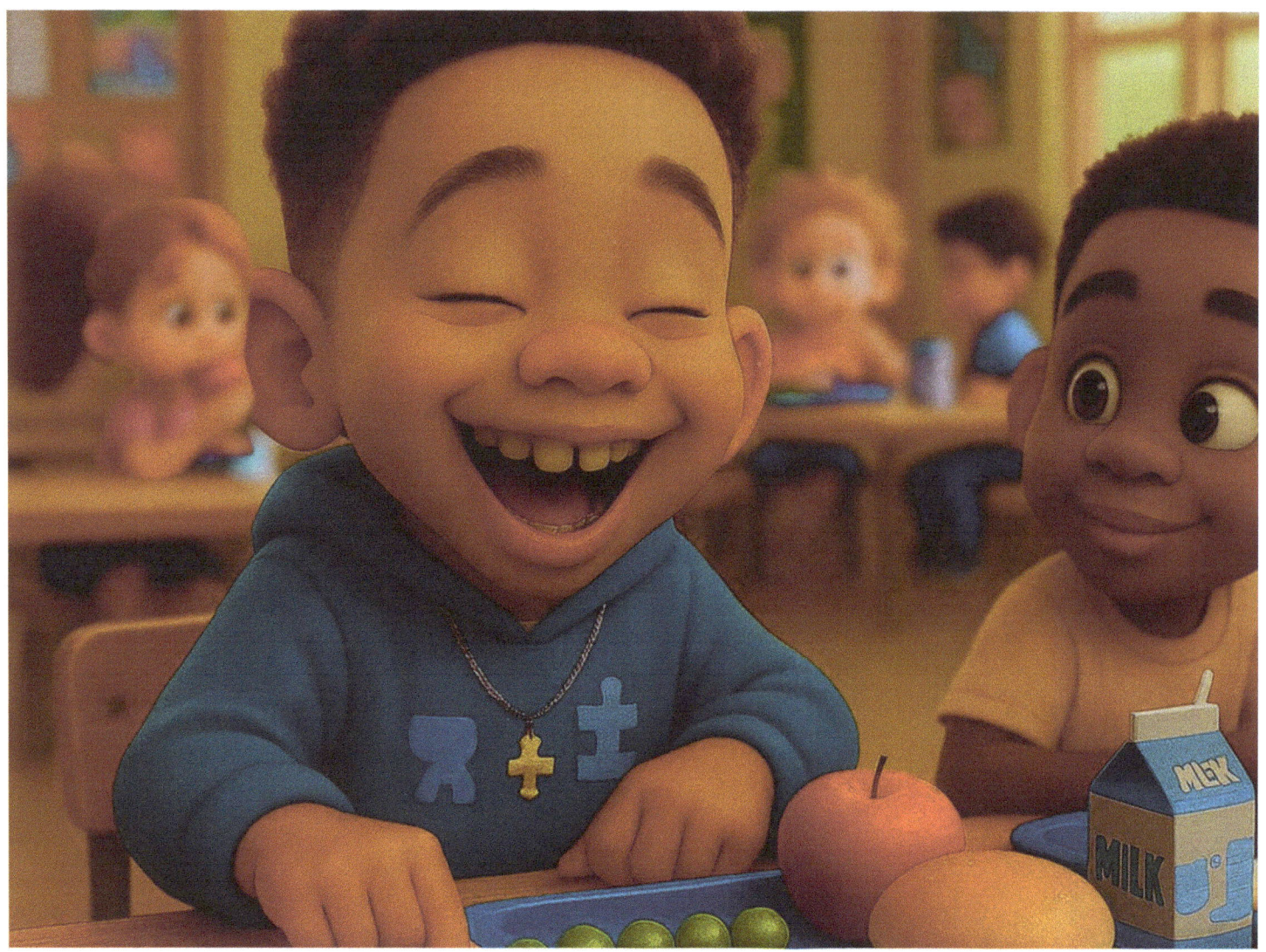

Today, something really cool happened. I made... a friend. A real one.
Not just someone who waves and walks away.
His name is Zion. He has a green backpack with a T-Rex on it.
Did I tell you I like T-Rex?

Zion talks fast, but I like it. He sat next to me at snack time.
I was lining up my grapes from biggest to smallest like always.
He didn't laugh.
He just said, "Cool. Can I help?"
No one ever asked if they could help me before.

I let him line up the apple slices. He got two out of order,
but I didn't tell him. Because he smiled so big.
And it felt nice to have someone sitting close who didn't make me feel weird.

At recess, he didn't run off. He stayed by me and said,
"Wanna dig for treasure?"
So, we dug a hole in the sand and pretended we found dinosaur bones.

It wasn't loud.
It wasn't too much.
It was just right.

When Mama picked me up, I told her,
"I made a friend today."
And her eyes got all shiny like she was going to cry,
but she smiled and said, "I knew you would."

-Show and Tell Day-

Today was Show and Tell day.
At first, I didn't want to do it.
Talking in front of people makes my words
feel stuck in my throat.
Like peanut butter with no jelly.
But the teacher said I could
bring anything I wanted.

So, I brought my rock. Not just any rock,
my special rock.

Did I tell you I like rocks?

It's smooth and round and gray with little
sparkles when the sun hits it.
I found it at the park with Mama.

It feels good in my hand. It helps
me when my brain gets too loud.
The other kids brought toys.
One boy had a robot that talked.
A girl had a doll with purple hair.

When it was my turn, I walked slowly to the front.
My tummy was doing flips. But I held my rock real tight.

I said,
"This is my rock.
It helps me feel calm.
It's quiet and heavy.
Like me."

Some kids blinked at me. One boy whispered, "That's not a toy."
But Zion said, "That's cool. It's like a superhero tool."
And just like that I wasn't scared anymore.
Because someone saw me. Really saw me.
Not just what I brought… but why I brought it.

After, the teacher said, "Thank you for being brave, JoJo."
And I smiled. Not big and loud.
Just enough.
Because I was brave.
Even if my voice was soft.

-The Day I Got in Trouble-

Today I got in trouble.
Like, real trouble.
My name was on the board with a sad face next to it. I didn't even know what I did wrong.

It started during reading time.
Did I tell you I like reading time?

The teacher said, "Sit criss-cross applesauce." But my legs didn't want to fold. They felt tight and twisty.
So, I laid on my belly instead,
it helped me think better.

The teacher said,
"JoJo, sit up like the others."
I tried. But my body didn't like it.
So, I rolled over, and my foot
bumped the bookshelf.

THUMP!
A stack of books fell.

Everyone looked at me.
Some kids laughed.
The teacher didn't.
She said, "That's enough, JoJo. You need to make better choices."

That word "choices" made my chest feel hot. I wasn't trying to be bad.
I was just trying to feel okay. But I didn't know how to say that.

Later, I had to sit by myself at lunch.
No talking.
No playing.
It felt quiet in the bad way.
When Mama picked me up, I told her what happened. I thought she'd be mad. But she knelt down and said, "Sometimes the world asks you to fit in a box. But baby, you were made to stretch past the edges."

Then she hugged me tight and said, "Next time, we'll help them understand your way too."

-Field Trip Day-

Today we went on a field trip!
We got on a real school bus.
It was loud and bumpy and smelled like
old crayons and peanut butter.
I didn't like the noise,
so I put on my headphones and looked
out the window.
The trees looked like
they were dancing.

We went to the science museum.
There were dinosaurs, space rockets,
and a giant bubble room.

Zion stayed close to me the whole time.
He said, "JoJo, let's go touch the
meteor rock!" I didn't want to—
so many people were crowding it.
So, instead, Zion and I sat
by the fish tank.
Did I tell you I like fish?

The jellyfish moved like
slow, glowing clouds.

Then something funny happened.
One of the girls screamed when the
T-Rex roared in the exhibit.
But I didn't even jump.
I just whispered, "He's not real. He just
wants to play." Zion laughed and said,
"You're braver than me!"

We ate lunch outside.
I had a juice box, apple slices, and a sandwich
with no crust.
I dropped my cookie in the grass,
but Zion gave me half of his.
He said, "That's what friends do."

On the ride home, I leaned against the window.
I didn't say much.
I was tired but happy.

New places make
my brain tired sometimes.
But today… it was a good kind of tired.

-The Day I Wanted to Quit-

Today I didn't want to go to school.
I pulled the covers over my head and told Mama,
"My brain feels too tired today."

She sat on the edge of my bed and rubbed my back.
I didn't cry. But I felt like it.
Not loud crying. Just the kind that lives behind your eyes.
Quiet and heavy.

At school, everything felt hard. The pencil didn't want to stay in my hand. The lights were buzzing again. I got one answer wrong and the boy next to me said, "Why are you even here if you don't get it?"

I wanted to quit. I wanted to go back to my soft place with Josie.
Did I tell you Josie is my best friend?
No bells. No stares. No "hurry up."
Just puzzles and peace.

But I didn't quit. I took deep breaths.
I looked at the wall until my body stopped shaking.
And when the teacher asked who wanted to help pass out papers,
I raised my hand. Even though it was shaking a little.

-Almost Time for Graduation-

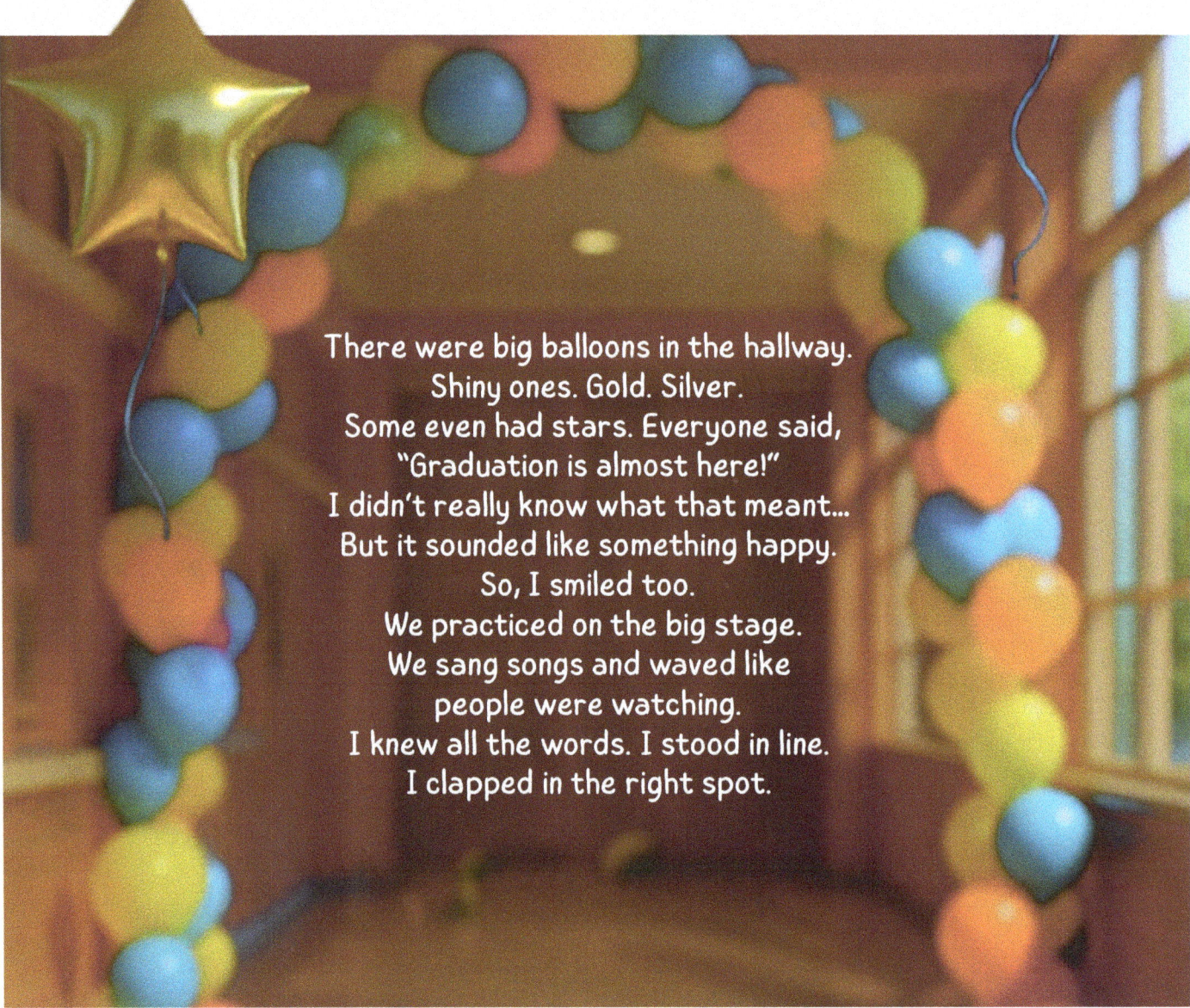

There were big balloons in the hallway.
Shiny ones. Gold. Silver.
Some even had stars. Everyone said,
"Graduation is almost here!"
I didn't really know what that meant...
But it sounded like something happy.
So, I smiled too.
We practiced on the big stage.
We sang songs and waved like
people were watching.
I knew all the words. I stood in line.
I clapped in the right spot.

I even helped Thomas when his paper hat broke. I thought I was doing good. I felt good. Then Mama picked me up early one day. She buckled my seatbelt real slow. She looked at me, but her eyes didn't smile.

"JoJo," she said real soft, "I want you to know I'm so proud of you."

My tummy started feeling funny.

When grownups say proud, I thought, something sad is coming.

She said, "The school thinks you should stay

in kindergarten one more year."

I blinked. **"But I practiced."** "I know, baby." **"I wore my star shirt."** "I know." **"I helped Thomas with his hat."** "You did. You were amazing."

I looked out the window and asked in a whisper,

"Do I still get to go on stage?"

Mama didn't say anything. She just looked out the window too.

And I knew the answer.

I didn't cry. I just pulled my hoodie over my head.

And looked out the window the whole way home.

My heart felt like it wanted to go hide under my bed.

-Graduation Day-

Today was graduation. But not for me. Mama didn't wake me up early.
There was no star shirt. No packed lunch. No bus.
I stayed home. I sat on the couch with my cereal and watched cartoons.
But they weren't funny today.

My belly felt too twisty for laughs.
Mama gave me extra syrup on my waffles.
She sat next to me real close. But her eyes kept checking her phone.
I think she didn't want me to see something.
Later, I peeked over her shoulder. I saw a picture. My class.
Standing in a line. Wearing the hats. The same hats we practiced in.

I saw Zion.
And Sam.
Even the girl who gave me her extra
crayons once. They were all smiling.
My chest got tight. Like someone put a big rock
inside it. I didn't say anything.
Just got up, went to my room,
and closed the door.

I put on my cape. The blue one Mama made from her scarf. I looked in the mirror and whispered, "It's okay, JoJo. You're still smart. You're still special."

My voice was wobbly. But I said it again anyway. Later, Mama came in and sat on the floor with me. She didn't say a lot. She just hugged me. A long, long time.

And in that hug, I knew something:
Even though I didn't walk across a stage, I still showed up this year.

Even when it was hard and that matters.

-I Thought I Was Going to First Grade-

After graduation day, I didn't talk much.
Mama said I could stay
home for the week.
No more songs.
No more loud bells.
Just quiet.
But my brain didn't feel quiet.
It was full of questions.
Like...
"Will I get a new teacher?"
"Will my desk be next to the
window again?"
"Do they have crayons in first grade?"

One morning, I finally asked.
I was sitting at the kitchen table
with my favorite blue cup.
Mama was washing dishes.
I said it real fast so I wouldn't get scared,
"Am I going to first grade?"

She turned off the water.
She turned around. And her face looked like it wanted to smile,
but it couldn't. "JoJo…" she said soft again. That soft voice again.

"You're going to do kindergarten one more time."
I looked down at my cup. I stared at the little superhero sticker
I put on it last month. I didn't say anything for a long time.
"But I already did kindergarten," I whispered. "I know, baby."
"I know all the shapes now." "You do."
"I can count to one hundred." "You're so smart, JoJo.
This isn't because you're not smart."

"Then why?"
Mama walked over and knelt beside me. She held my hand.
"Because sometimes your brain needs a little more time.
And that's okay."

But it didn't feel okay. It felt like my heart dropped through my socks.
I wanted to scream. But I didn't.
I just sat there with my superhero cup. Trying to feel brave.
But instead… I felt like I disappeared.

My Name is JoJo.
I didn't walk on stage.
I didn't wear the hat.
And I didn't go to first grade.
But you know what?
I still showed up.
I still tried.

I still kept going.
Even when my brain got tired.
Even when my hands
dropped things.
Even when the noise felt
too loud and the world
felt too fast.

I stayed.
I breathed.
I wore my cape.
Some days I still feel wobbly inside. Like Jell-O.

Some days, I get mad at my brain for being different.
I cry sometimes.
But then I remember what Josie says:
"JoJo, your brain is magic. It sees things other people miss.
It feels things really big. That's not a mistake.
That's a superpower."

And Mama says,
"Different doesn't mean broken, baby. It means brave."
So, I believe them.

My name is JoJo.
I'm kind.
I'm funny.
I love stars, puzzles, and blue capes.
And even if the world doesn't always understand me...
I understand me.
And that's enough.

About Josiah (JoJo)

Josiah is six years old… and a walking miracle.
At just two years old, he was diagnosed with Level 3 severe autism by two developmental pediatricians.
They said he'd never talk.
They said the odds were against him.
But Josiah didn't just defy the odds—he destroyed them.

Today, Josiah attends private school in North Carolina, surrounded by two active, determined parents and four big brothers who pour nothing but love, structure, and belief into him every single day.

And the boy who was never supposed to speak?
He's now reading at a second-grade level and solving math problems with his peers.

Josiah is proof that labels don't define potential.
He's not just an inspiration — he's the blueprint.
The blueprint for what happens when early intervention meets fierce love, relentless faith, and a village that refuses to give up.

"They said he'd never talk. Now he's reading, counting, and showing the world who he is. I always believed in my baby. And I always will."
— Nastasja K, Proud Mom

This is JoJo. And he's just getting started.

About the Author

Nastasja K. is a mother, military leader, and fierce advocate for neurodivergent children. With over 17 years of active-duty service in the United States Armed Forces, she balances duty, discipline, and deep compassion in every part of her life, especially motherhood.

As a proud mom of five boys, Nastasja's world shifted when her middle son Josiah was diagnosed with autism at just two years old. Through his eyes, she began to see the world differently, more sensitively, more honestly, and more beautifully.

My Name is JoJo was born from that vision: a story that honors the brilliance, bravery, and unique perspective of children on the spectrum.

Nastasja writes to help families feel less alone, to empower educators with understanding, and to bring visibility to the children who often go unseen. Her mission is clear through storytelling; she builds bridges between awareness and acceptance, difference and dignity.

Because different isn't less.
It's powerful.
And so is her voice.

Be on the lookout for other My Name is JoJo Books:

My Name is JoJo – Meet My Best Friend Josie

My Name is JoJo – I'm a Big Brother Again